SCIENCE GETS PHYSICAL

Physical Science in
SNOW AND ICE SPORTS

COOK MEMORIAL LIBRARY DISTRICT
413 N. MILWAUKEE AVE.
LIBERTYVILLE, ILLINOIS 60048

ENZO GEORGE

CRABTREE
PUBLISHING COMPANY
WWW.CRABTREEBOOKS.COM

Author: Enzo George
Editors: Sarah Eason, Jennifer Sanderson,
    and Elizabeth DiEmanuele
Consultant: David Hawksett
Editorial director: Kathy Middleton
Proofreader: Wendy Scavuzzo
Design: Paul Myerscough and Jeni Child
Design edits: Katherine Berti
Cover design: Lorraine Inglis
Photo research: Rachel Blount
Print and production coordinator:
    Katherine Berti

Written, developed, and produced by Calcium

Photo Credits:
Inside: Inside: Shutterstock: aiyoshi597: p. 31; Diego Barbieri:
p. 36, 37; Olga Besnard: p. 33; Paolo Bona: p. 38; BrunoRosa:
p. 40; Marc Bruxelle: p. 7; DarioZg: p. 35; Denim Background:
p. 44; Alt Eduard: p. 41; Eric Fahrner: p. 42; Vladislav Gajic:
p. 43; Giorgiomtb: p. 13; Gorillaimages: p. 9; Peter Gudella:
p. 45; Mitch Gunn: p. 8, 10; Brendan Howard: p. 18; Andrea
Izzotti: p. 29; Jag_cz: p. 6; Herbert Kratky: p. 39; Krumcek: p.
17; Lightpoet: p. 32; Lopolo: p. 5; Geir Olav Lyngfjell: p. 12;
Mjaud: p. 22; Nickolya: p. 21; Alexander Rochau: p. 11, 14; Jeff
Smith – Perspectives: p. 27; Sportpoint: p. 15; B.Stefanov: p.
30; StockphotoVideo: p. 3; Thiti Sukapan: p. 24; Testing: p. 34;
Merkushev Vasiliy: p. 19; Dusaleev Viatcheslav: p. 20; Zastolskiy
Victor: p. 16; Dmytro Vietrov: p. 4; Leonard Zhukovsky: p. 1,
23, 28; Wikimedia Commons: 121a0012: p. 25, 26
Cover: Shutterstock: Resilva

Library and Archives Canada Cataloguing in Publication

Title: Physical science in snow and ice sports /
  Enzo George.
Names: George, Enzo, author.
Description: Series statement: Science gets physical |
  Includes index.
Identifiers: Canadiana (print) 20190195452 |
  Canadiana (ebook) 20190195460 |
  ISBN 9780778775478 (hardcover) |
  ISBN 9780778776505 (softcover) |
  ISBN 9781427125224 (HTML)
Subjects: LCSH: Winter sports—Juvenile literature.
Classification: LCC GV841.15 .G46 2020 |
  DDC j796.9—dc23

Library of Congress Cataloging-in-Publication Data

CIP available at the Library of Congress

LCCN: 2019043463

Crabtree Publishing Company
www.crabtreebooks.com   1-800-387-7650

Printed in the U.S.A./012020/CG20191115

Copyright © **2020 CRABTREE PUBLISHING COMPANY**. All rights reserved. No part of this publication may be reproduced, stored in a
retrieval system or be transmitted in any form or by any means, electronic, mechanical, photocopying, recording, or otherwise, without the
prior written permission of Crabtree Publishing Company. In Canada: We acknowledge the financial support of the Government of Canada
through the Canada Book Fund for our publishing activities.

Published in Canada
Crabtree Publishing
616 Welland Ave.
St. Catharines, Ontario
L2M 5V6

Published in the United States
Crabtree Publishing
PMB 59051
350 Fifth Avenue, 59th Floor
New York, New York 10118

Published in the United Kingdom
Crabtree Publishing
Maritime House
Basin Road North, Hove
BN41 1WR

Published in Australia
Crabtree Publishing
Unit 3 - 5 Currumbin Court
Capalaba
QLD 4157

CONTENTS

CHAPTER 1

IT IS COLD!

What do you think of when you think of winter? Do you ski, toboggan, or watch hockey on television? If you do, you are also a **physics** fan! Everything that happens in winter sports can be explained by the laws of physics.

Free Moving

Winter sports started in cold places that have snow and ice most of the year. They started as ordinary ways to travel, such as using skis, sleds, or skates to travel over snow and ice. Almost all winter sports involve overcoming the **force** of **friction**. Friction is created when one surface rubs against another. Skiing, sliding, and skating all depend on reducing friction as much as possible.

Unlike a skateboard, a snowboard is attached to the rider's feet. This makes it easier to do tricks.

On the Snow

Skiing is a method of traveling over snow by wearing a pair of long skis. The skis help prevent the wearer from sinking into the soft snow. There are two main types of skiing: alpine and Nordic. Alpine, or downhill, involves racing down steep slopes and uses the force of **gravity**. Nordic, or cross-country, skiers use a different technique to travel over flatter terrain.

In recent decades, there has also been the growth of snowboarding. Riders use a short wide board with rounded ends to race, and perform aerial tricks. Snowboarding is based on skateboarding. The physics of both are very similar.

On the Ice

Tobogganing with friends is a lot of fun, but sledding can also be a serious sport. Three Olympic sports involve racing downhill on pairs of **runners**. Bobsleds have crews of two or four people.

They race in sleds that have bodies of carbon fiber and other tough materials. In skeleton bob, also known as skeleton, a competitor rides a flat sled head first. In luge, the slider lies on their back and travels feet first.

Ice skates were one of the earliest methods of traveling on frozen lakes and rivers. Today, people compete in figure skating on ice rinks. They carry out jumps and twists, and more artistic ice dancing. There is also speed skating. These skaters are less interested in looking good, but instead skate for speed. Skating is also the basis of hockey, the most popular winter team game.

There are many ways to have fun on the ice. But, be prepared to fall over more than once!

Snow and Ice

Snow and ice are frozen forms of water, but they do not have much else in common. Both snow and ice vary in their qualities. Winter sportspeople need to pay attention to the exact conditions to get the very best performance.

Changing Snow

When it first falls, snow is mostly powdery and dry. It is made up of individual drops of water that have frozen into crystal flakes. They clump together as they fall. Fresh fallen snow is full of air, like a sponge, which makes it soft. Skis are long because they spread the weight of the skier out to prevent them from sinking into the soft snow. However, as more snow falls, the lower layers of snow are **compacted**, so the air is pushed out and the snow becomes harder. If the temperature falls, the remaining water turns to ice, so the snow becomes solid and glassy. That makes it far more slippery than fresh snow.

When snow is fresh and dry, the skis send the top layer into the air as clouds of powder.

The blade of an ice skate scrapes sideways on the ice as the skater comes to a stop.

Melting Snow

Snow and ice both have less friction than the ground, so it is easier to slide across them. In fact, skiers, sliders, and skaters do not actually touch the snow or ice itself. While both surfaces have low friction, there is still enough to slow athletes down. The law of the **conservation** of **energy** says that energy cannot be created or destroyed.

If the athlete slows down, that energy has to go somewhere else. In this case, it is converted to heat between the bottom of the skis, runners, or skates, and the frozen surface. This heat melts a very thin layer of water **molecules** on the top of the snow or ice. So, the athlete is actually moving over a liquid rather than a solid.

GETTING PHYSICAL: ON ICE

Ice is water that has frozen solid. It is normally colder than snow, and can be as hard as stone and as smooth as glass. Its surface is so smooth that it offers very little friction in the form of grip for the bottoms of normal shoes. The colder the ice, the less friction it has, so the quicker runners and skates can slide over it. Warmer, softer ice is slower.

7

CHAPTER 2

SKIING

The most famous of all sports on snow is probably skiing. Competitors wear a long, thin ski on each foot. They use them to slide over the snow, usually carrying long poles in each hand to balance themselves. Skis look simple, but they are carefully designed for their purpose.

Built for Speed

Skiers can be at many levels of ability. They can be young beginners on bunny slopes or experts competing at the Winter Olympic Games. They all have the goal of reducing friction so they can slide easily over the snow. But, they can do this in different ways. Some skis are longer and have straighter sides. The length helps the skier travel fast.

A skier heading straight down a hill can achieve incredibly high speeds, but that is highly dangerous and difficult to control. So, in the first half of the 1900s, skiers began to travel in a series of zigzags. Long skis are more difficult to turn. Shorter skis that are slightly thinner in the middle are easier to use. They can help skiers make tighter turns.

Skiers turn around bends by leaning over to dig the edges of the skis into the snow.

In a field of fresh snow, skiers transfer their weight rhythmically from side to side to travel in a series of curves.

Ski Engineering

The first skis were up to 8 feet (2.4 m) long. They were little more than narrow planks of wood that skiers attached to their feet with tape. Now, skis are highly engineered pieces of equipment. They are made from layers of different materials, such as fiberglass, wood, aluminum, glue, and artificial, or humanmade, substances called polymers. The layers bend and stretch to different levels. So, the skis are **flexible** enough to absorb pressure from bumps in the snow but stiff enough to carry a skier around a bend. Turning involves digging the sides of the skis into the snow. The ski has to be stiff enough to keep its shape.

The skier's ankles are supported by high plastic boots. This helps them control the skis by leaning. It also helps avoid broken ankles if they fall. The boots clip into brackets on the ski, so the skier's feet are completely anchored. That gives the skier added stability.

Velocity and Drag

Snow is slippery. That is why it is such fun to slide over. High up at ski resorts, there are often spectacular views out over mountain scenery, with huge fields of snow and perhaps small towns and villages far down in the valleys. Downhill skiers can reach high speeds and feel the wind whistling past as they whiz through the clean air. All this enjoyment is because of the principles of physics.

Moving Fast

The point of alpine skiing is to get down the side of a mountain as quickly or enjoyably as possible. This is usually achieved by pointing skis downward and letting gravity do the rest. On a straight run down a steep slope, however, a skier can **accelerate** to a **velocity**, or speed, of up to 150 miles per hour (241 kph). That is far too dangerous for most people. Instead, skiers pass from one side of the hill to the other and travel diagonally down the mountain.

Skiers adopt a tuck position, with their body low and their poles under their arms. This lessens the area of their body that is affected by **air resistance**, or **drag**.

Steady Progress

A skier crouches to keep their **center of mass** low. A low center of mass keeps air resistance low and reduces the effect of **torque**. Torque can push the skier's body backward and cause them to fall as their legs slip forward. Another reason skiers should bend their legs is so their knees can act as shock absorbers. This technique can help soften the **impact** of skiing over uneven ground. It also means that the skis can stay in contact with the snow as much as possible. This contact helps the skier maintain **momentum** and keep control. If the skier takes off into the air, they have no way to change their velocity until they land again.

While snow has low friction, there are many forces resisting the skier's motion. The first is how deep a skier sinks into the snow on their skis. Usually, this friction affects skiers in areas of fresh snow. The snow gets compacted as they pass over it. Another type of friction is caused by the thin layer of water that forms beneath the skis. Water in the snow clings to the bottom of the ski and stretches, slowing it down. This is called **capillary** drag. Another cause of friction is the base of the ski rubbing the snow, which causes static electricity. The charge attracts grit to the ski and makes it move slower over the snow.

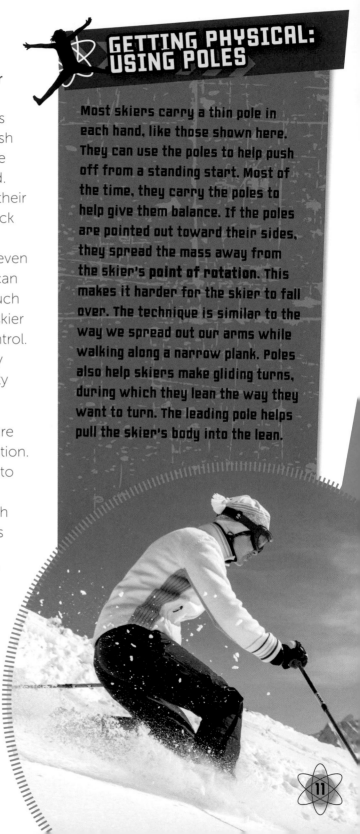

GETTING PHYSICAL: USING POLES

Most skiers carry a thin pole in each hand, like those shown here. They can use the poles to help push off from a standing start. Most of the time, they carry the poles to help give them balance. If the poles are pointed out toward their sides, they spread the mass away from the skier's point of rotation. This makes it harder for the skier to fall over. The technique is similar to the way we spread out our arms while walking along a narrow plank. Poles also help skiers make gliding turns, during which they lean the way they want to turn. The leading pole helps pull the skier's body into the lean.

11

Carving and Edges

Sooner or later, all skiers have to turn. It is too dangerous to go hurtling straight down the side of a mountain. The low friction means that a skier would accelerate to such a velocity that any fall could be fatal. Mountains can also be dangerous places. They have drops, trees, chair lifts, and other obstacles. If you want to ski fast, you have to be able to avoid dangers.

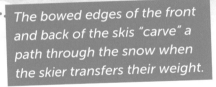

The bowed edges of the front and back of the skis "carve" a path through the snow when the skier transfers their weight.

Steering a Line

Skis steer when the skier moves their center of mass to change the way their skis run across the snow. When people start to ski, they use snowplow turns. They point the front ends of their skis together, which tilts each ski toward its inward edge. The skis move at an angle over the snow. The skier leans one way, and digs one edge in more than the other, so the skier will turn in that direction. More experienced skiers use parallel turns. Parallel turns are when their skis remain parallel throughout the maneuver. Again, they steer by placing more weight on one ski or the other by moving their bodies. They hold out their arms and bend their knees. This time, they lean so that the inside edge of one ski and the outside edge of the other ski both catch the snow at once. This causes the skier to turn toward the outer edge. Moving their weight in a regular rhythm lets the skier glide down a slope in a series of S-bends.

Turning Circles

Skis are long, so they do not turn cleanly on the snow. Long skis have a wide turning circle. To turn in a shorter distance, the edges must not cut into the snow in a regular curve. Instead, they must alternate between cutting into the snow and skidding over the surface. They do so in a series of short slides. This alternation causes added friction on the bottom of the ski. The friction slows a skier down while they are turning.

The answer to this problem came from snowboarding. Snowboarders made shorter boards cut with a narrow waist so, they were shaped a little like an hourglass. They had a tighter turning circle than skis. The cut-out on the sides and at the front and back allowed them to stay carved into the snow throughout a curve. Skiers did the same. Today, most skis are a little shorter than they used to be, and narrow in the middle rather than at the ends.

GETTING PHYSICAL: SLIDING ON WAX

Skiers put wax on the bottom of their skis to help them slide. They also add it for grip. In alpine skiing, wax helps reduce the amount of water the ski forms. It also prevents the bottom of the ski from absorbing too much water from the snow. But, if too little water forms at the top of the snow, increased friction slows down the ski. Skiers choose harder or softer wax to match the conditions such as the temperature and type of snow. Cross-country skiers use grip wax designed to add friction to the base of their skis. This friction helps them use their skis to push themselves forward.

Technicians use hot irons to melt different types of wax onto the bottom of a ski. Then they plane and polish it until it is absolutely smooth.

Cross-Country Skiing

One of the most popular forms of skiing is Nordic skiing, which is also called cross-country skiing. It is one of the oldest ways of traveling across snowy landscapes.

Get a Grip

Unlike downhill skiers, cross-country skiers cannot rely on gravity. They often have to travel uphill, not just over a flat surface. They have to push themselves along using their skis and poles. Alpine skis are designed to slide over the snow with as little friction as possible. Cross-country skis are designed both to glide and to provide grip when it is needed.

In classic cross-country technique, the skier slides each ski forward. The skier follows a pair of channels carved into the snow. The skier should not be able to move forward. It is very slippery. They should simply slide back and forth. But, the skis are designed to provide more or less friction at different stages of movement. This design helps them move forward.

The classic technique of cross-country skiing involves the skier raising and lowering each ski alternately to glide over the snow.

Skiers use their skis in a "herringbone" shape to push themselves uphill without losing energy by slipping backward.

Ski Design

Nordic skis are cambered, or built so that the middle bows up from the ends. As the skier glides along, the middle part of the ski is not in contact with the snow. When the skier pushes back, all their body weight is placed on that ski. This pushes the middle section down into the snow to provide more grip. The middle section of the ski can be roughened with wire to provide more grip. It can also be coated with special wax to increase friction, but that sometimes makes crystals of snow cling to the wax. Snow can form clumps on the skis that slow the skier down. Snow crystals have sharper, more jagged edges in colder temperatures.

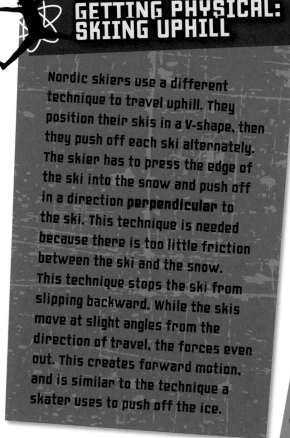

GETTING PHYSICAL: SKIING UPHILL

Nordic skiers use a different technique to travel uphill. They position their skis in a V-shape, then they push off each ski alternately. The skier has to press the edge of the ski into the snow and push off in a direction perpendicular to the ski. This technique is needed because there is too little friction between the ski and the snow. This technique stops the ski from slipping backward. While the skis move at slight angles from the direction of travel, the forces even out. This creates forward motion, and is similar to the technique a skater uses to push off the ice.

Ski Jumping

One of the most spectacular forms of skiing involves moving through the air. Ski jumpers slide down an artificial slope, gaining speed until they hit the end of the ramp and take off. The aim is to fly as far as possible, then land cleanly on the snow. This follows the natural path of the jumper through the air.

Maximum Speed

The length of the jump depends on the jumper's velocity through the air. The greater the velocity, the longer the jumper can stay in the air before gravity pulls them back to the ground. There are two ways of reaching the greatest velocity. The first is to gain maximum speed on the ramp. The second is by adopting an **aerodynamic** shape through the air to minimize air resistance, or drag.

On the ramp, the skier keeps their skis in parallel channels. These channels are carved into the snow. Touching the sides will slow down the skis. The skier also crouches to reduce the front area that is heading into the wind, which also reduces drag. By the time the skier reaches the table, or takeoff area, they will have accelerated to a speed of around 60 miles per hour (97 kph).

A ski-jump ramp is 295 feet (90 m) long, rising to 393 feet (120 m) for large-hill competitions.

Hinged brackets for the front of the feet allow ski jumpers to raise their heels and lean forward almost parallel to their skis.

In the Air

In the air, ski jumpers take an aerodynamic position. They lean forward as flat as possible, so they are traveling nearly parallel to the ground. The skier also spreads their skis in a V-shape. This shape cuts down the area of the frontal surface, reducing air resistance. It also provides **lift**, which holds the jumper a little bit longer in the air. They can then travel a farther distance before touching down. While it seems as though ski jumpers are very high in the air, the shape of the hill actually follows their path. This means the skier does not land with too much vertical impact. Instead, they land with **linear momentum** that they can reduce once their skis are on the ground. A ski jumper is only ever about 12 feet (3.7 m) above the ground, but that is probably too high for many people!

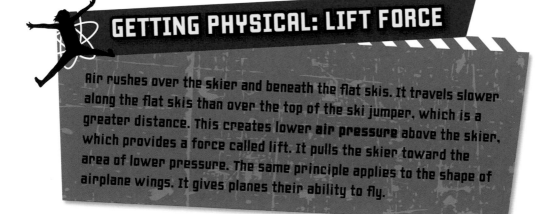

GETTING PHYSICAL: LIFT FORCE

Air rushes over the skier and beneath the flat skis. It travels slower along the flat skis than over the top of the ski jumper, which is a greater distance. This creates lower air pressure above the skier, which provides a force called lift. It pulls the skier toward the area of lower pressure. The same principle applies to the shape of airplane wings. It gives planes their ability to fly.

CHAPTER 3

SNOWBOARDING

What does a snowy mountainside have in common with the waves crashing on the beach? Physics! People ride over the snow and through the surf using boards. These boards are very similar in their design and how they work.

Snow and Surf

The first snowboards were created in the 1960s. A father tied two skis together to make a toy for his daughters. His new creation looked like a surfboard. He called it a "snurf," a combination of "snow" and "surf." The new sport gained followers over the 1970s and 1980s. In the mid-1970s, snowboards were being made with better mechanisms to hold the feet in place. At the beginning, skiers dismissed snowboarders as unskilled. Snowboards were banned from many ski areas. However, the new sport grew fast and by the early 2000s, virtually all ski resorts had separate areas for snowboarders. They also had **halfpipes**, ramps, and rails for doing tricks.

Snowboarders use features such as rails and ramps to kick them into the air to perform tricks.

Snowboarders developed a wide range of aerial tricks. Some of them were later copied by skiers.

New Generation

Most of the new riders were young. They were eager to do more than just ski down hills. Snowboards could slide over the snow like skis, but their larger surface area created more friction. The rider's position was less aerodynamic than a skier's tucked position. That meant snowboards were not as quick going downhill as skis. But, snowboarders soon realized that they could do many things skiers could not. They could jump more easily and perform stunts, such as skimming along rails raised above the snow. By launching themselves off ramps and halfpipes, snowboarders could perform aerial tricks. This opened a whole new world of winter sports.

Many snowboarding tricks were based on skateboarding. Boarders in both sports learned the benefit of small changes and physics. Changes to their boards, such as curves cut into the sides of snowboards, could increase their tricks. These could help the riders gain more grip with the edges at the front and back of the board, so they could turn through tighter circles.

Jumps

Snowboards are great for doing tricks. They ride down U-shaped tubes called halfpipes, crossing from side to side. They can also race down a hillside. They launch themselves from kickers, or ramps that throw them into the air. They do spins and twists before they land on the snow.

Using Momentum

The time a snowboarder has to perform tricks in the air is set by their velocity. The slope at the top of the ramp is at a steep angle, so it throws them up into the air. The rider's **kinetic energy** carries them up as well as forward. As they slow down, gravity pulls them back to the ground. Their path through the air is a smooth **arc**.

To spin and twist in the air, the snowboarder needs both linear momentum and angular momentum. Angular momentum is the energy that causes the body to rotate and continue rotating, such as in a head-over-feet somersault. This is related to the rider's angular velocity, or how fast they spin. To create angular momentum, the snowboarder needs to create torque as they leave the ramp. It is not possible to generate torque once in the air.

How long a boarder has to turn somersaults depends on their linear momentum (or velocity x mass) as they leave the ground.

GETTING PHYSICAL: HANG TIME

Snowboarders can do more spectacular tricks if they spend longer in the air. They try to achieve as long a "hang time" as possible. On a big jump from a ramp, that might be 3 seconds. To pull off spectacular tricks, they need to hit the ramp at about 40 miles per hour (64 kph). They rotate on takeoff by twisting their midsection and crunching their abdomen. Once in the air, they crouch and grab their board with one hand. This crouch lowers their **moment of inertia**, which makes them rotate faster. As they pull their arms to their chests again, their spin speed increases. Then they throw out their arms to stop themselves spinning, ready to land.

Bending the legs or pushing them out straight affect the way the body moves through the air.

Moment of Inertia

Once they are in the air, snowboarders change the shape of their bodies to alter their movements. The rider can change their angular velocity, or how fast they spin, by changing their moment of inertia. This is the object's rotational mass, which is the property of the object that makes it more difficult to turn. The higher an object's moment of inertia, the harder it is to make it turn. The moment of inertia depends not just on an object's mass, but on its position relative to the point of rotation. The farther a mass is from the point of rotation, the higher its moment of inertia.

When the snowboarder somersaults, the point of rotation is near the center of their body. If they tuck their arms and legs close, more of their mass is closer to the rotation point. This tuck lowers the moment of inertia, which speeds up the rate they spin.

Halfpipe

The halfpipe is a U-shaped channel carved into the hillside. While the halfpipe runs straight down the hill, snowboarders go down in zigzags. They shoot up the steep sides and over the lip to perform tricks. Since they travel in zigzags, they do not gain full velocity from the force of gravity. They have to create their own momentum.

Gaining Energy

In a halfpipe, snowboarders need to gain speed so they can shoot up over the lip to perform tricks. It is difficult to push off the curved ground with their feet, so they do this by pumping. As the board crosses the flattish bottom of the U-shaped tube, the rider crouches down. Then, they straighten up and raise their arms as the board reaches the bottom of the sloping wall. This increases the rider's energy and makes the board travel faster. By pumping during a run, a rider can increase velocity.

A rider shows the bottom of their board as they grab the edge during a jump.

SCIENCE WINS!

CHLOE KIM'S GOLD MEDAL

U.S. snowboarder Chloe Kim got a lot of attention at the 2018 Winter Olympics. In the photo below, she is mid-run on the halfpipe at the games. The games were in Pyeongchang, South Korea, the country from which her parents had emigrated. Although she was only 17, Kim handled the pressure well.

On her first run on the halfpipe, Kim had a near-perfect run. Although she slipped on her second, by her third, she had already won gold. Kim celebrated by performing back-to-back 1080s. Each one has three complete revolutions in the air. She began rotating as she reached the lip of the pipe. Then, she reached down with one hand to grab her board and speed up her spin. The key was landing the first 1080 cleanly. Without a perfect landing, she would have lost too much speed to be able to pull off the second jump.

Making an Effort

As the board begins to curve upward, **centripetal force** pulls the rider down toward it. This means the rider needs more energy to straighten up. The work of straightening up gains a little energy for the board and rider. It helps them travel faster. It takes some effort from the rider because of the resistance of the centripetal force. In physics, that effort is evidence that they are doing "work," or using forces. The effect is similar to swinging your legs at the bottom of a swing's arc to "kick" the swing higher. In this case, the snowboarder gains height above the lip. This lets them perform tricks in midair.

23

CHAPTER 4

SLIDING SPORTS

In countries with a lot of snow and ice, people have always used sleds to move around. Sleds usually have parallel runners in place of wheels to move smoothly over the surface. Sledding downhill has evolved into three main sports: bobsledding or bobsleigh, skeleton, and luge. Official sled races usually take place on tracks up to 1.1 miles (1,760 m) long, with up to 20 tight **banked** curves. The tracks are concrete channels, which are permanently coated in ice, thanks to a refrigeration system in the walls. All three sliding sports are very fast! A four-man bobsled can reach speeds of 84 miles per hour (135 kph).

You do not need a proper toboggan to slide down a hill. Some people use inner tubes, serving trays, or even thick sheets of plastic or polythene.

Bobsleds

Bobsleds have two parallel sets of runners. These are divided into steerable front sections and fixed rear sections. They have a shell made of light materials, which helps make sure the sled's center of mass is as low as possible. This makes it easier to steer the sled and keeps it from spinning out on steep curves. The shells are tested in wind tunnels to reduce the amount of air resistance, or drag, they experience.

In the past, Team USA Olympic bobsleds have been designed by engineers who design NASCAR race cars. They use the same aerodynamics to achieve the least drag. Bobsled teams have two or four members. In a two-person team, the first athlete is the driver or pilot who steers. The second uses the brake to stop the sled at the bottom of the run. In a four-person team, there are two more pushers who get the sled moving.

Luge and Skeleton

On the luge, one or two athletes travel feetfirst, lying on their backs. They steer by pushing against the fronts of their runners with their calves. They also shift their shoulders and body weight to help make small changes in direction.

Skeleton is short for skeleton bobsled. Sliders lie on a flat sled and travel headfirst down the track. The frame and runners of the sled must be made of steel. The base plate is often made of plastic to keep it light. There is no steering mechanism. The slider steers by creating torque, or rotating force, by moving the position of their head, shoulders, and feet. Skeleton is the slowest of the three sliding sports. It is slow because the headfirst position causes more resistance. That may be a good thing, because the skeleton has no brakes.

Skeleton sliders keep their arms along their body as they slide. They bring them forward at the end of their run to press down on the sled to help slow it down.

Fastest Start

Whether you are on your toboggan or racing for gold, the physics are the same. The quicker you can get the sled sliding over the ice, the more velocity you will gather as you move. You can achieve the same goal by reducing forces that slow you down, such as air resistance and friction.

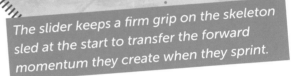

The slider keeps a firm grip on the skeleton sled at the start to transfer the forward momentum they create when they sprint.

Saving Time

In competitions, timing is vital. Top races take place over two runs down the track. The two times get added together. The winning places are often separated by as little as one-tenth of a second. Every fraction of a second is the difference between winning and coming in second.

Once the sled is in motion, it is powered by gravity. Gravity pulls all the sleds down the track with the same acceleration. It is important to get the most acceleration possible at the start. The English scientist Isaac Newton's Second Law of Motion says

force = mass x acceleration. The mass of all bobsleds is evened out by using weights so that it is the same for everyone. That means the only way to achieve more acceleration is to increase the force applied to the sled at the start through the push by the athlete or athletes.

These athletes can run and push the sled up to 164 feet (50 m) along the track before getting in. They use spikes on their shoes to grip the ice. Some teams use Olympic sprinters to push. These sprinters can generate more force than most runners.

Bobsleds, luges, skeletons, and toboggans face two kinds of resistance: One from the snow or ice under the runners and another from the air. The runners are thin. This is to reduce friction with the ice, while also offering enough grip for small trenches as they slide. Sliders reduce air resistance by the smooth, skin-tight bodysuits they wear. They also take on an aerodynamic position. In the bobsled, everyone keeps their heads as low as possible inside of the shell. On the skeleton and luge, sliders keep their bodies flat and their arms and legs as straight as possible and tight to their bodies.

Getting an Advantage

For skeletons, the slider runs as hard as possible at the start. Then, they fling themselves down onto the sled. On luges, the sliders start in a sitting position. To move the luge, they have to overcome static friction, the force that keeps objects at rest. They overcome friction by pushing against the ice as hard as they can with the spiked gloves they wear on their hands.

Sliders hope to gain an advantage. If they manage a clean run, they should be able carry that advantage to the finish line!

Handles fold out from a bobsled to give athletes something to push against. This makes sure all the motion pushes the sled forward rather than sideways.

The Perfect Line

Bobsled takes its name from the way the heads of the racers seem to bob around as they speed down the track. This may appear random, but in fact, everyone onboard is helping to steer. They use their weight to move the sled one way or the other.

Riding Along

A push athlete on a bobsled team has just 164 feet (50 m) at the top of the run to make the sled move as fast as possible. Most of these push athletes are outstanding sprinters and the sled is lightweight, so this takes only five seconds. Once the push athlete has jumped onto the sled, the hard part of his job is done. Now the driver takes over to steer the perfect line down the track. However, the other athletes still have a role to play. They tuck down low, beneath the sides of the sled. This keeps drag from air resistance to a minimum. As the sled banks around turns, they also move their body weight from side to side or back and forth. Moving their weight helps keep the sled's center of mass in a place where it will cause the least friction.

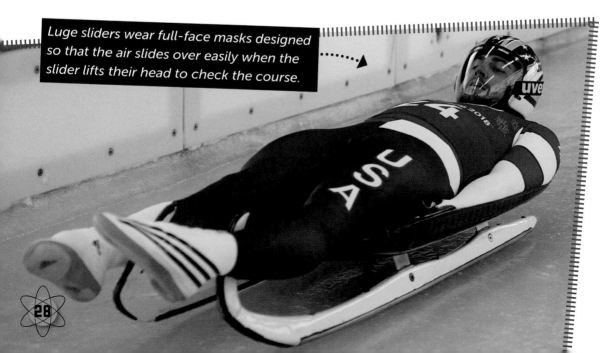

Luge sliders wear full-face masks designed so that the air slides over easily when the slider lifts their head to check the course.

Steering the Sled

The driver or pilot is the most important member of the team. They hold two rings attached to the front runners by wires and pulleys. The driver needs to find a perfect line down the course. They have to avoid any bumps on the ice walls that cause friction that can slow down or knock over the sled.

When the front runners are not exactly parallel to the sled's direction, they turn sideways to the sled's progress. This creates more friction. The driver tries to steer as little as possible. Just turning the runners a fraction too far one way or the other can lead to disaster.

On a skeleton, athletes steer by moving their body weight on the sled. Their legs trail behind them and act as a **rudder**. If the athlete moves their legs one way, the sled turns the other way. On a luge, the athlete squeezes the front of the runners with their calves to steer the sled.

Steering the sled requires a high degree of skill, as the runners can easily catch in the ice during a turn and pull the sled off course.

GETTING PHYSICAL: CENTRIFUGAL FORCES

In a bobsled run, as the sled speeds through one of the banked turns, the driver has to pick the best line. The ideal line is high enough to keep up the sled's momentum, but not so high it has to travel farther. The sled is pushed up toward the top of the banking by centrifugal force, which is related to inertia. Inertia is a moving object's tendency to keep moving in a straight line, unless it is acted on by another force. When a sled turns, its inertia tries to keep it moving on its straight line. That has the effect of throwing the sled and its riders toward the outside of the turn. This is the danger point on any run.

29

CHAPTER 5

ICE SKATING

Five thousand years ago, the first people skated across the ice. They strapped wooden blades to their feet. Skating is still popular, especially in colder countries. In these countries, rivers and lakes freeze in the winters.

Moving Fast

Skating has created different sports. One is speed skating in which skaters race with each other for a set distance on an oval track. Long track speed skating takes place over greater distances. Short track speed skating takes place on a very small oval with tight curves. In speed skating, there are many falls. Hockey is another kind of skating. This is a team sport played by using long sticks to try to get a puck into the opposition's goal.

Short track speed skaters wear special gloves with reinforced fingertips to help them steady themselves as they turn tight corners.

For most people, the ice rink is a fun place to hang out with friends and family.

ROCK CENTER CAFÉ

...and Moving Beautifully

The other major form of ice skating is figure skating in which an individual or pair of skaters perform a routine to music. The routine includes skating, as well as jumps and twists. Pairs skating also bring in lifts in which one skater raises their partner high above their head. Another kind of figure skating is ice dancing, which was inspired by ballroom dancing. It is always performed by pairs, but does not have jumps or lifts. Instead, the performers concentrate on the rhythm and emotions of the music. A final version of figure skating is **synchronized** skating. This kind of skating marks competitors on how well timed the team members are in their movements.

Gliding Along

All skating depends on the same physical forces to allow skaters to glide over the ice. Skate blades lack friction because they are thin, and because the skates and the ice are very hard and smooth. After using friction to get themselves moving, skaters use this lack of friction to be able to glide. As they glide, they are subject to Newton's First Law of Motion. This law says that an object in motion will tend to remain in motion until it is affected by another force, such as gravity. This quality is known as inertia. Since the friction on skates is so low, a skater sliding across the ice tends to keep going. They keep going unless they change direction.

Blades and Weight Distribution

If you have ever been to an ice rink, you will remember how unsteady you felt when you first tried skating. The blades are very thin, so they reduce the area through which your mass passes to the ground, which makes them unstable. The blades are as long as, or longer than, the length of your feet but not as wide. This is why new skaters often extend their arms as far as they can for balance. They might not know it, but they are trying to reduce their moment of inertia to help them stay upright.

The skater's weight is concentrated on the small area of the skate that is in contact with the ice. This creates friction that cuts a groove and melts the upper layer of the ice.

Stay Upright

An object's moment of inertia is a measure of how easy or difficult it is to make that object rotate around an **axis**. The lower the moment of inertia, the easier it is for the object to rotate. When you are skating, the pivot of this rotation is your feet. If you overbalance, your feet stay in place while your body rotates. By putting out your arms to the sides, you are moving some of your mass away from the pivot point. Moving your mass away from this point raises the moment of inertia. This makes it harder for you to rotate and overbalance. You can see the same principle in other ways, such as when people walk across a narrow log and hold their arms out at their sides or when tightrope walkers carry long poles.

Pushing Off

Newton's Third Law of Motion says that for every action, or force, there is an equal and opposite reaction. This lets a skater push across the ice. If the skater pushed off a foot with the skate parallel to the direction of travel, their foot would just slip. There would be no friction to stop it. Instead, the skater turns their foot outward as they prepare to push off, or take a "stroke." When they put down their foot, it is at an angle of about 45 degrees to the direction of travel. At that angle, the side of the blade bites into the ice, which provides enough friction for the skater to push off. A skater slides along in a series of slightly diagonal pushes that add up to forward velocity.

Modern skates have sharp metal blades that are fastened to the bottoms of special boots. There is little flexibility in the blades. They are so sharp, they have to be covered with plastic guards to move around off the ice. Otherwise, they would cut into the floor.

SCIENCE WINS!

VANESSA AND MORGAN'S RECORD DANCE

In 2018, at Skate Canada International, the French pair of Vanessa James and Morgan Ciprès gained record scores. These scores were in the short program and the free-skating program. They won the gold medal with a new record total score. Their programs included complex throws. Ciprès helped James to take off from the ice and perform three full twists in the air. The jumps, which include lutzes and axels, have to be accurate to score well. For each, the jumper has to take off from a particular part of the edge of one of their blades. Then, they land on another specific edge.

Perfect Spin

There are some amazing moves in figure skating. They include forward and backward somersaults, and triple axels.

A skater who keeps their trailing leg extended in a camel spin turns faster as they lower their leg and raise their upper body. This reduces their moment of inertia.

In the Air

Skaters lift off the ice at about 10 miles per hour (16 kph) and can jump up to 4 feet (1.2 m) in the air. The more vertical velocity they can get from their jump, the more time they have to perform their tricks. The more linear momentum and rotational speed they have, the larger their angular momentum. Angular momentum lets them spin faster in the air. Skaters who jump 4 feet (1.2 m) in the air have a "hang time" of up to 1 second. But, because their average jumps are only 2 feet (60 cm), they usually have a hang time of 0.7 seconds to carry out spins.

By increasing the velocity of their takeoff, some can do quadruple (4) spins. This requires an average rotational spin of about 340 revolutions per minute (rpm). A quintuple (5) spin would need a spin speed of almost 500 rpm. The record is around 440 rpm. So, quintuple spins are beyond the ability of humans and the laws of physics!

One question many people wonder about ice skaters is how they avoid getting dizzy when they make rapid spins. The organs that control our balance are tiny channels inside our ears that contain fluid and many sensitive hairs. When the fluid moves as our bodies move, the hairs detect movement and send instructions to the brain to make whatever movements are necessary to keep us balanced. When our heads spin, the fluid at first gets left behind. Then, it catches up and rotates at the same speed as the head. This can make it seem as though you are still and the rest of the world is turning around you. When you stop, however, the fluid keeps moving for a while—and that is what makes us dizzy. Skaters cannot avoid this feeling, because their bodies always obey the laws of physics. They simply have to train until they get used to it!

Tornado on Ice

One of the most spectacular maneuvers in skating is the long spin. Skaters revolve fast in one place on their skates. They speed up as they rotate. They look a little like a tornado on the ice! When a skater starts a spin with their arms extended, they have a high moment of inertia. Inertia resists angular momentum, or speed of rotation. As the skater spins, they bring their arms closer to their body. This move decreases their mass and moment of inertia, but the spin's angular momentum continues. Angular momentum comes from multiplying the moment of inertia by the angular velocity. If the moment of inertia decreases, the angular velocity must increase, so the skater spins faster.

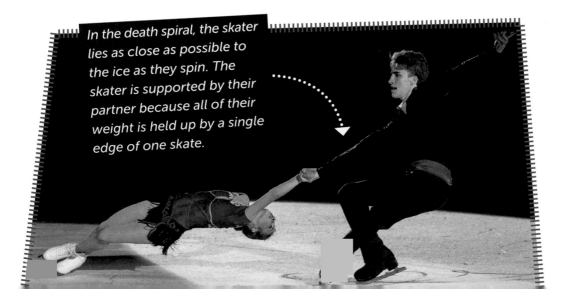

In the death spiral, the skater lies as close as possible to the ice as they spin. The skater is supported by their partner because all of their weight is held up by a single edge of one skate.

Speed Skating

As its name suggests, speed skating is all about going as fast as you possibly can. Skate races take place over various distances on long track courses. These have long straights and U-shaped curves, like running tracks and short track courses. These are tight courses that are only 36 feet (11 m) in diameter. Races are fast and furious. There are many crashes, as skaters battle for the inside of the curve, which is the shortest way around the track.

Laws of Motion in Action

Speed skaters show all three of Newton's Laws of Motion. Once they are moving, they stay in motion until an external force makes them stop. That is the First Law. There are many crashes in short track speed skating. The external force might be the side of the ice rink. Newton's Second Law is that force = mass x acceleration.

A skater with a heavier mass will have to create more force than other skaters to get the same acceleration. The Third Law is that for every action, there is an equal and opposite reaction. That describes what happens when the skater pushes backward with their foot. The opposite force of the ground pushes them forward.

Short track speed skaters all try to hug the inside line of the bends, because it is the shortest route around the course.

Use Your Arms ...and Your Head

Since speed skaters wear skates, they cannot push straight backward with their feet. Instead, they have to turn them outward at a diagonal angle so the edges of their skate catch in the ice and push them forward. Speed skating is series of slightly diagonal motions, so skaters use their arms to help keep them heading in a straight line. On each push, they swing one arm out behind them. This creates a force in the opposite direction that balances the sideways push of the skate. In long races, speed skaters sometimes place both their arms behind their backs. This is mainly to save energy for later in the race. Swinging your arms is hard work. It is like pumping your arms up and down when you run. Skaters keep their bodies pushed forward. This position helps their balance and keeps their backs parallel to the floor. This reduces drag from the air, similar to the smooth body suits they wear.

When a skater leans too far, their mass no longer presses down through the skates, which can slip out from beneath the skater and cause a crash.

GETTING PHYSICAL: STAYING UPRIGHT

Skaters on the short track lean over at angles of less than 45 degrees. They often have to put down their inside hand on the ice to help steady them. At such an angle, they look as though they will fall over. Sometimes, they do. The sharp edge of their skate blade bites into the ice. It carves a curved trench that steers the skate around the bend and also prevents it from slipping. As the skater turns, they are stopped from flying outward by centripetal force. This is the force that pulls an object traveling around the outside of a circle toward the center of the circle. It helps short track racers stay on their feet.

CHAPTER 6

HOCKEY

Hockey is the national sport in Canada. It is the second most popular sport in Russia after soccer. National Hockey League (NHL) and Stanley Cup matches are broadcast around the world.

Physics in Action

While an NHL match sometimes can be hard to follow, with physics, it is very clear. Hockey is a demonstration of basic laws. The sticks move the puck forward, moving kinetic energy from the players' muscles to the puck. This transfer lets players move the puck very fast. As skaters travel, they gain high amounts of linear velocity. The lack of friction acting on their blades lets them travel faster than a run—forward and backward.

Forward and Backward

When hockey players skate, they turn their skates diagonal to the direction of travel. They push off the back foot, while the front foot slides forward. They then repeat the action on the other foot. This is a demonstration of Newton's Third Law. The force with which the player pushes backward is met by an equal and opposite force, which pushes them forward. When they travel backward, hockey players keep their feet parallel on the ice in a series of shallow S-shaped curves. During each curve, they push against the ice with the outside of their skate blades to keep up their momentum. That way of pushing themselves does not generate the same amount of force as skating forward, so skating backward is always slower.

Players' lower legs are padded to protect them from sharp skate blades and hard sticks.

Hollow Blade

To give players the best grip on the ice with little friction, hockey skate blades are about 0.1 inch (0.25 cm) thick. They have a hollow along the middle that creates two sharp edges on each side of the blade. These sharp edges can bite into the surface of the ice, which makes it easier to stop and turn. It also helps with gaining explosive bursts of acceleration to chase after the puck. A slip at the wrong time could give away possession and lead to a crucial goal being given away.

Crouching down lowers the body's center of mass. This makes it harder to be pushed over in a tackle.

Playing with Levers

There is a reason why hockey goalkeepers wear lots of protection. The puck hurtles toward them at up to 100 miles per hour (160 kph). The puck is a rubber disk 1 inch (2.5 cm) thick that weighs 6 ounces (170 grams). It is frozen hard before play to reduce bouncing on the ice. It can do a lot of damage to the human body.

Multiplying Energy

The speed at which a puck can travel has to do with the length of the hockey stick. A stick is like a long **lever**, with its **fulcrum** in the player's shoulder. A lever is a machine that multiplies force. The distance the stick travels in the player's hands translates into a much longer distance at the tip of the stick. The length can be almost as long as the player is tall. This means the blade of the stick is traveling far faster than the player's hands, so it strikes the puck with more energy.

Just before a slapshot, the stick bends back in a bow against the ice. As it straightens, it transfers that **potential energy** to the puck in much the same way as a bow transfers energy to an arrow.

The multiplying force of the stick can be increased by the amount of flex in the stick. A more flexible stick can bend before it strikes the puck. It stores up potential energy that creates kinetic energy. This is particularly true of the slapshot. The slapshot was invented in the early 1900s. It made the most of the physics behind the hockey stick. Potential energy is energy possessed by an object because of its mass and position. It can become kinetic energy.

SCIENCE WINS!

DENIS'S FASTEST EVER HOCKEY SHOT

The fastest-ever recorded hockey shot was a slapshot hit by Denis Kulyash. Playing in an All-Stars skills competition in St. Petersburg, Russia, Kulyash hit the puck at a 110.3 miles per hour (177.5 kph). Such high speeds are usually only achieved in skills competitions. The player needs to be able to concentrate and go through a full wind-up with his stick. In a real game, there is rarely enough time for that. Players are too busy looking for a pass or shot, or trying not to get tackled.

The slapshot is the fastest of all hockey shots. It can be used only when a player has time to go through the full motion. The player lifts the stick up over their shoulder and pulls it back. Then, they bring it down to strike the ice just before the puck. The stick stops and bends as the player's hands keep moving forward. This stores kinetic energy in the stick as potential energy. As the player shifts their weight and flicks their wrists, the stored energy is released from the stick as it makes contact with the puck. The energy turns back to kinetic energy.

Crash!

Hockey can get rough. Players crash into one another all over the ice as they try to win the puck. Even fans get excited when the players crash each other into the screens around the rink. Sometimes, this leads to fights on the ice. Such a physical sport requires that players wear protective gear such as helmets and pads.

Tackle with Torque

A main force involved in body checks and other contact tackles is torque, or rotational force. There is a lot of torque involved in hockey. Players create forward force and, as this happens, their bodies tip backward around a point of rotation near their waists. Players crouch forward as they set off to stop their upper bodies from rotating backward.

One way to tackle is to push the player into the wall, using momentum to increase the force of impact.

In a hockey collision, torque helps knock players off their feet. The point of rotation of an object is always near its center. So, hitting a player high or low is the easiest way to generate torque. Low tackles are illegal in hockey. Players hit higher up, around the chest and shoulders. This drives the upper body back, so torque forces the legs to swing forward and knocks the player off their feet. Players can try to resist this by lowering their center of mass as much as possible. The center of mass is where the body is most stable.

The Force of Speed

The force of a tackle or body check is determined by the player's mass and acceleration. Newton's Second Law of Motion says: force = mass x acceleration. A smaller player skating faster can generate the same force in a tackle as a larger player moving slower.

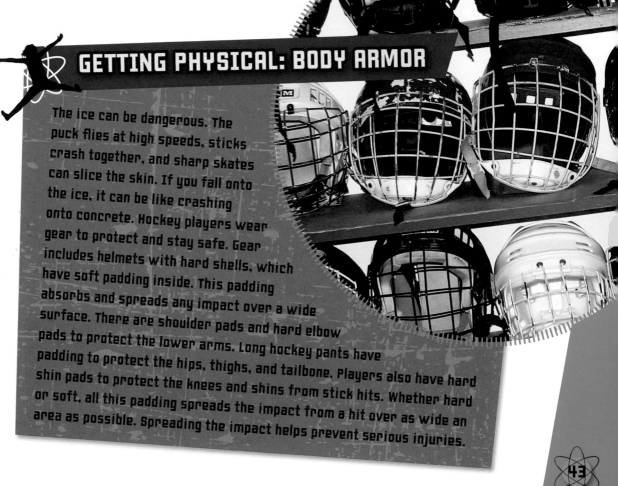

GETTING PHYSICAL: BODY ARMOR

The ice can be dangerous. The puck flies at high speeds, sticks crash together, and sharp skates can slice the skin. If you fall onto the ice, it can be like crashing onto concrete. Hockey players wear gear to protect and stay safe. Gear includes helmets with hard shells, which have soft padding inside. This padding absorbs and spreads any impact over a wide surface. There are shoulder pads and hard elbow pads to protect the lower arms. Long hockey pants have padding to protect the hips, thighs, and tailbone. Players also have hard shin pads to protect the knees and shins from stick hits. Whether hard or soft, all this padding spreads the impact from a hit over as wide an area as possible. Spreading the impact helps prevent serious injuries.

GET PHYSICAL!

It is time to find out for yourself something about the science of winter sports. In this experiment, you will learn about friction. The experiment is more fun if you do it with a friend, but you can also do it on your own.

YOU WILL NEED:

- Smooth wooden plank or floorboard
- Wax (paraffin wax, candle wax, or ski wax)
- Ruler
- Video camera or phone camera
- Ice cubes
- Masking tape

Instructions

1. Prepare the plank or board. Leave one side as smooth wood and apply wax to the other side. Rub the wax all over to make sure the wood is fully covered and that the wax is smooth to the touch. You can scrape away bumps with a butter knife, then rub with a cloth to smooth out the surface.

2. Find a position on the floor or a table next to a wall. Use a strip of masking tape and the ruler to mark a scale of inches (cm) on the wall, starting with zero at the level of the floor or table.

The snowplow position, in which the skis are turned inward in a v-shape, prevents even the most slippery skis from sliding over the snow.

3. Lay the plank along the floor or table so that one end is directly in front of your scale or ruler. Make sure the camera is set up so it can film the plank.

4. With the unwaxed wood facing upward, place an ice cube near the end of the plank. Lift that end of the plank slowly into the air until the ice cube starts to slide. Use your scale to record how high you had to lift the plank.

5. Repeat the experiment.

6. Flip the plank over and try the same experiment on the waxed surface. You may need to use a fresh ice cube if the first one is starting to melt. Record how high you had to lift the plank before the ice cube started to slide.

7. Repeat the experiment.

8. Watch your results on video. It might help to watch on a large screen.

Analysis

On which side of the plank did the ice cube start to slide first? Why do you think that might be?

Conclusion

You probably found that you had to raise the plank higher on the unwaxed side to make the ice cube move. This is because of friction.

When the plank is flat, the ice cube is held in place by its inertia. Inertia is the tendency of an object that is still to remain still unless a force sets it in motion. As you raise the plank, the force of gravity begins to pull the ice cube down. However, the ice cube is held in place by friction. How much resistance a surface has is called its coefficient of friction. Plain wood has a higher coefficient of friction than wax. Wax is smoother, so the ice slides over it more easily. That is why downhill skiers apply wax to the bottom of their skis. This practice helps reduce the friction between their skis and the snow.

GLOSSARY

accelerate To change velocity by speeding up, slowing down, or changing direction

aerodynamic Designed to reduce drag from the air

air pressure The force exerted onto a surface by the weight of air

air resistance A force that acts in the opposite direction of an object traveling through the air, slowing it down

arc A smooth curve

axis An imaginary line around which an object rotates

banked With tilted sides around a curve

capillary Relating to thin tubes, such as the gaps between grains of snow

center of mass The point in the middle of an object's mass

centrifugal force A force that pushes a revolving object toward the outside of its spin

centripetal force A force that pulls a turning object toward the rotation point

compacted Tightly packed

conservation Staying constant

drag A force that opposes an object's motion

energy The capacity for doing work

flexible Able to bend easily

force An interaction that changes the motion of an object

friction The resistance of one object moving over another

fulcrum The point against which a lever is placed to turn

gravity A force that attracts things toward the center of Earth, or toward any other physical body

halfpipes Wide trenches with curved bases and steep sides

impact The action of one object hitting another

inertia The quality of a moving body that makes it stay in motion or in a stationary body that makes it stay still

kinetic energy The energy an object has because of its motion

lever A bar resting on a pivot or fulcrum, used to move loads

lift A pulling force generated by lower pressure above an object

linear momentum The amount of forward motion of an object

mass The quantity of matter in an object (its "weight")

molecules Particles formed by atoms bonding together

moment of inertia A measure of resistance to rotational movement

momentum The quantity of motion of a moving body, a product of its mass and velocity

perpendicular At a right angle to something

physics The branch of science that studies materials and energy

point of rotation The point around which an object turns

potential energy The energy possessed by an object because of its mass and position

rudder A flat piece of wood or metal, moved to control direction of travel

runners Long, thin strips of wood or metal

synchronized Happening at the same time

torque The force that causes objects to rotate

velocity Speed in a specific direction

LEARNING MORE

Find out more about the physics of snow and ice sports.

Books

Abramovitz, Melissa. *Skiing* (Science Behind Sports). Lucent Books, 2014.

Hile, Lori. *The Science of Snowboarding* (The Science of Speed). Capstone Press, 2014.

Ventura, Marne. *STEM in Figure Skating* (STEM in Sports). Sportszone, 2017.

Winters, Jaime. *Carve it Snowboarding* (Sports Starters). Crabtree Publishing, 2012.

Websites

Find information about hockey, with details about the science behind it, at:
https://adventure.howstuffworks.com/outdoor-activities/ snow-sports/hockey1.htm

Understand the science behind the Winter Olympics by watching video clips at:
http://nbclearn.com/olympics/cuecard/47275

Discover facts about how skaters move on slippery ice at:
www.real-world-physics-problems.com/physics-of-ice-skating.html

Read a scientific analysis of the perfect bobsled run at:
https://ssec.si.edu/stemvisions-blog/perfect-slide-science-bobsledding

INDEX

Cook Memorial Public Library

3 1122 01570 9905

JUL 2 2 2020

P9-CMW-378